INDIA

LETTERS FROM AROUND THE WORLD

David Cumming

CHERRYTREE BOOKS

LETTERS FROM AROUND THE WORLD

Titles in this series

BANGLADESH · BRAZIL · CHINA · FRANCE · INDIA · ITALY · JAMAICA · JAPAN · KENYA · SPAIN

A Cherrytree Book

Conceived and produced by

Nutshell
MEDIA

Intergen House
65-67 Western Road
Hove BN3 2JQ, UK
www.nutshellmedialtd.co.uk

First published in 2003 by
Evans Brothers Ltd
2A Portman Mansions
Chiltern Street
London W1U 6NR

© Copyright Evans Brothers 2003

Editor: Katie Orchard
Designer: Tim Mayer
Map artwork page 5: Encompass Graphics Ltd
All other artwork: Tim Mayer
Geography consultant: Jeff Stanfield, Geography
   Inspector for Ofsted
Literacy consultant: Anne Spiring

All photographs were taken by David Cumming.

Printed in Hong Kong

VISIT OUR WEBSITE
www.evansbooks.co.uk
Evans

Acknowledgements
The author would like to thank the following for their help
with this book: the Menon family; the principal, staff and
pupils of Vidyodaya School, Kochi; Rajinie Singh, Renuka
and the staff of the Kochi office of Beeyu Plantations Ltd.

British Library Cataloguing in Publication Data
Cumming, David, 1953-
   India. – (Letters from around the world)
   1. India - Social conditions - 1947 - Juvenile literature
   2. India - Social life and customs - 20th century -
   Juvenile literature
   I. Title
   945'.052

ISBN 1842341421

Cover: Lakshmi, Nithin and a friend.
Title page: Lakshmi and her friends set off on a bike ride.
This page: The city of Kochi.
Contents page: Taking an auto-rickshaw to school.
Glossary page: Lakshmi plays with her friends.
Further information page: Lakshmi reads in her room.
Index: Lakshmi on the climbing frame at Maria Park.

Contents

My Country

Monday, 7 January

15 Paramara Street
Edapally
Kochi
Kerala,
India 862173

Dear Sam,

Namaste! (This means 'hello' in Hindi.)

My name is Lakshmi Menon and I'm 9 years old. I live in Kochi, on the coast of Kerala, in India. Look on the map to see where Kochi and Kerala are. Being your pen-pal is a great idea – I'll be able to help you with class projects on India.

Write back soon!

From

Lakshmi

Here I am with Dad, Mum and my brother, Nithin – he's 11 years old.

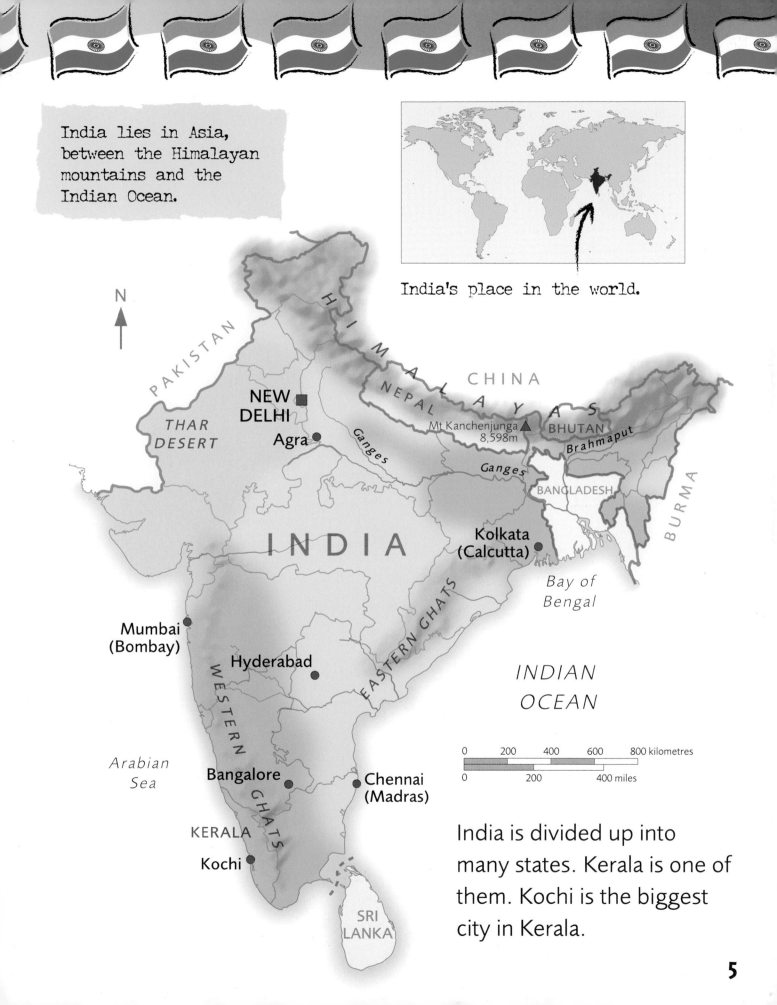

India lies in Asia, between the Himalayan mountains and the Indian Ocean.

India's place in the world.

India is divided up into many states. Kerala is one of them. Kochi is the biggest city in Kerala.

5

Kochi is a very busy place. About 800,000 people live there. Kochi is the most important city in Kerala because it has a large port. Ships from all over the world take away coir, rubber, tea and spices from Kerala.

Like most Indian cities, Kochi's streets are always busy with traffic.

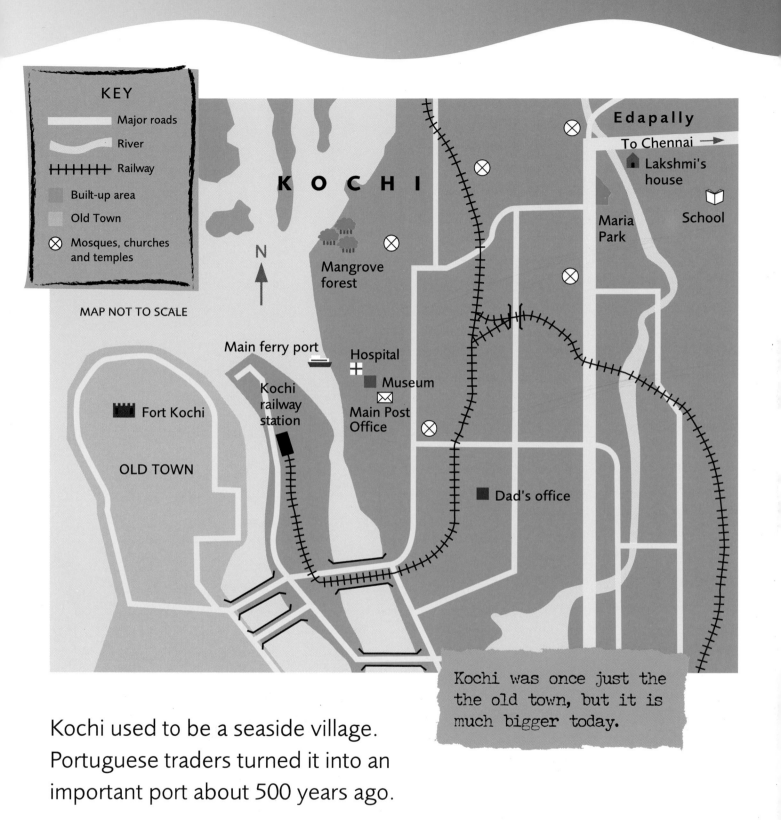

KEY

Major roads
River
Railway
Built-up area
Old Town
⊗ Mosques, churches and temples

MAP NOT TO SCALE

N

K O C H I

Mangrove forest

Edapally

To Chennai →

Lakshmi's house

Maria Park

School

Main ferry port

Hospital

Museum

Kochi railway station

Main Post Office

Fort Kochi

OLD TOWN

Dad's office

Kochi was once just the the old town, but it is much bigger today.

Kochi used to be a seaside village. Portuguese traders turned it into an important port about 500 years ago.

Lakshmi lives in an area called Edapally, in north-east Kochi. Once it was a separate village. But the city of Kochi has grown so much that Edapally is now part of it.

Landscape and Weather

Kerala is squeezed between hills, called the Western Ghats, and the Arabian Sea. It is criss-crossed by many rivers flowing down from the hills into the sea.

Kerala is very flat and full of trees. Bridges have been built to cross its many rivers.

North India has high mountains and a big desert. The mountains are cold and wet. The desert is hot and dry. Kochi is hot all year round. A wind called the monsoon brings a lot of rain between May and October.

Kochi's Climate

January	July
Temperature	Temperature
27°C	26°C
10mm Rainfall	572mm Rainfall

Lakshmi often needs an umbrella to keep dry during the rainy season.

At Home

Lakshmi lives in a house that was built four years ago by her parents. Her Grandma Kochammini lives there, too. Lakshmi's other grandparents, Grandad Achuthan and Grandma Indira, live just around the corner.

Grandma Kochammini has lived with Lakshmi's family since her husband died.

This is Lakshmi with her mum and brother, Nithin, in front of their house.

When the Menon family moved here many years ago there were few houses. Today there are homes everywhere. There is no empty land left on which to build any new buildings.

Lakshmi in her bedroom. She shares this room with Nithin.

Lakshmi and her friends like to play outside in the front yard.

Lakshmi's house has two floors. On the ground floor there are two lounges, a kitchen, a dining-room and Grandma Kochammini's room.

Upstairs there are two bedrooms, each with its own bathroom, and a study.

This is Lakshmi's dog, Jackie. The dog lives in a big kennel outside.

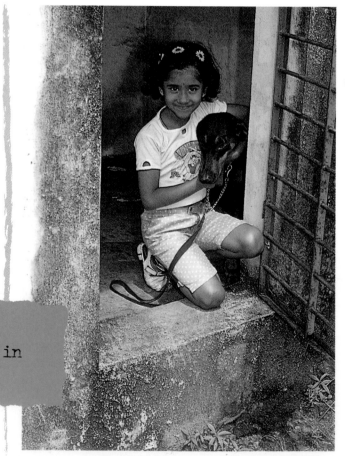

Tuesday, 12 March

15 Paramara Street
Edapally
Kochi
Kerala
India 862173

Dear Sam,

Thanks for your letter, which arrived last week. Have I told you about Grandma Kochammini? She lives with us. Most families in India have a relation living with them. Do your grandparents live with you? Grandma Kochammini has food ready for us when we get back from school, starving! She's teaching me how to cook. I might send you a recipe next time.

From

Lakshmi

Here I am helping Grandma Kochammini cook a meal.

Food and Mealtimes

Lakshmi begins her day at 6 a.m. with a *dosa*, a kind of pancake, for breakfast. Sometimes she also has an *idli*. This is a sticky ball of rice that is eaten with a bowl of *sambar*, a vegetable soup flavoured with tamarind. For lunch Lakshmi has rice and curried vegetables, or sandwiches.

Lakshmi helps Grandad Achuthan buy some fresh vegetables at the local market.

India's climate is hot enough to grow bananas. This banana tree is in Lakshmi's garden.

At about 7.30 p.m. she eats *chapattis* or *dosas* and a potato or vegetable curry for dinner. The Menons do not eat meat, and most of their food is fresh.

The Menon family has *dosas* for dinner.

Friday, 2 May

15 Paramara Street
Edapally
Kochi
Kerala
India 862173

Hi Sam!

I promised I'd send you a recipe – here's how to make *dosas* :

You will need: 295g long-grain rice, 75g *urad dhal*, water,
½ teaspoon fenugreek spice, pinch of salt, vegetable oil

1. Soak the rice in a bowl of water for 8 hours, and soak the *urad dhal* in another bowl of water.
2. Drain the rice and grind it in a blender for 3 minutes, then stir in 4 tablespoons of water to make a smooth paste.
3. Drain the *urad dhal* and grind it in the blender for 5 minutes with the fenugreek. Stir in 4 tablespoons of water to form a paste.
4. Mix the rice and *urad dhal* paste together and add the salt.

I'm checking
the mixture's
thickness here.

5. Cover and leave for 12 hours. (The mixture should double in size.)

6. Grease a griddle pan and heat it up. Spoon enough of the mixture on to the pan to cover it.

The dosa mixture hardens in the griddle pan.

7. When the batter has thickened, dribble some oil on to it and then flip it over. (Mum always does that bit for me.)

8. In 2 minutes the *dosa* is ready to eat.

Try them and let me know what you think.

Lakshmi

Two dosas ready for eating – delicious!

School Day

This is Lakshmi's school bus.

Lakshmi and Nithin go to the Vidyodaya School, which is about 8 kilometres away from Edapally. Most of the pupils use the school's buses to get there. They pick up children from all over Kochi. Lakshmi catches a bus every morning at 7.20 a.m.

There are 27 children in Lakshmi's class.

Most schools in India are state schools and are free. The Vidyodaya School is a private school so Lakshmi's mum and dad pay for her and Nithin to study there.

These children go to another school in Kochi. They travel there in an auto-rickshaw.

Lakshmi's school library has books in Hindi, India's main language, and other languages.

The school year begins in June and ends in March.
Then there is a long holiday in April and May.
Children begin school when they are 6 years old.
They leave when they are 17 to go to
college or university.

These boys are practising for the school basketball team.

Wednesday, 17 July

15 Paramara Street
Edapally
Kochi
Kerala
India 862173

Hi Sam,

Thanks for your last letter. You wanted to know what I do at school. This is what happened today:

8.00–8.30 a.m. Assembly	12.00–12.40 p.m. Singing
8.30–9.25 a.m. Science	12.40–1.25 p.m. Mallayalam
Break	(Kerala's language)
9.30–10.30 a.m. Maths	Break
10.30–11.30 a.m. English	1.30–2.10 p.m. Games
Lunch	2.10–2.50 p.m. Hindi
	Home time!

My favourite lesson is Science because we learn such interesting things with our teacher. What's yours?

From

Lakshmi

My teacher plays a harmonium in our singing lessons.

Off to Work

Lakshmi's mum teaches English at the Vidyodaya School. She travels on the school bus every day.

Lakshmi's dad sells medical equipment to hospitals. His office is in Kochi but he travels all over Kerala for his job. He takes the train on these trips and stays away for several days.

Lakshmi's dad at his office in the city centre.

In Kerala many things are still made by hand. This man is making furniture from bamboo.

Most people in Kerala are farmers. They grow rice, coconuts, spices, fruit and vegetables on their land.

This man earns money ironing people's clothes.

Free Time

Sunday is the only day when the whole family is together. Lakshmi's mum and Grandma Kochammini cook a delicious meal. Lakshmi's dad plays an instrument called a harmonium. He is teaching Lakshmi to play, too.

Lakshmi often plays on the climbing frames in Maria Park, near her home.

Lakshmi likes to take her dog,
Jackie, for a walk at weekends.

Nithin's favourite game is Carom.
This is a traditional Indian game.
It is played with counters on a
board with holes at each corner.
The aim is to flick the counters
into the holes.

Each player has eight
counters at the start
of a game of Carom.

Religion

Lakshmi prays at a Hindu shrine.

Most Indian people follow Hinduism, but there are many other religions in India.

Lakshmi and her family are Hindus. They have a shrine at home where they say prayers at 6 p.m. They also visit a temple in Kochi once or twice a month.

Christians worshipping at a church near Lakshmi's home.

Friday, 6 September

15 Paramara Street
Edapally
Kochi
Kerala
India 862173

Dear Sam,

It's so exciting here at the moment – we're celebrating Onam, our harvest festival. This is the most important festival in Kerala. Everyone is on holiday and there are parties with lots of wonderful food. There will be fireworks tonight.

I wish you could see them, too!

Love

Lakshmi

We made this pattern with flower petals outside our house for Onam.

Fact File

Capital city: New Delhi. It is called 'new' because it was built specially by the British to be India's capital. It became the capital city in 1911.

Other major cities: The largest city in India is Mumbai (once called Bombay), followed by Kolkata (Calcutta). Chennai (Madras) and Hyderabad are also large cities.

Neighbouring countries: Pakistan, Nepal, Bhutan, China, Bangladesh, Burma, Sri Lanka.

Size: 3,287,263km². India is the sixth-largest country in the world.

Population: 1 billion. India's population is the second largest in the world. (China has the largest population.)

Languages: Hindi and English.

Main religions: Hinduism is the largest religion in India. About 82 per cent of the people follow it. Islam is the next most important, with 12 per cent, and then Christianity, with 2 per cent. The rest of the people follow religions such as Sikhism, Buddhism and Jainism.

Flag: The orange stands for India's Hindu people. The green stands for its Muslims. The white in between stands for the hope that the Hindus and Muslims can live together happily. The wheel in the centre is an old symbol for peaceful change.

Currency: Indian rupee (divided into paise. 100 paise=1 rupee). Indian notes often have a picture of Mahatma Gandhi on one side.

Famous buildings: The Taj Mahal in Agra is one of the world's most beautiful buildings. It was built by the Emperor Shah Jahan in memory of his wife, Mumtaz Mahal. It took 17 years to build and was finished in 1653.

Famous people: Mahatma Gandhi was born in 1869. He is known as the 'Father of the Nation' because he helped India to become independent from British rule. He was killed in 1948.

Main industries: Iron and steel, clothing, jewellery, handicrafts.

Highest mountain: Kanchenjunga (8,598m) is on the border between India and Nepal. It is the third-highest mountain in the world.

Longest river: The River Ganges (2,655km). Hindus believe that the Ganges is a holy river, so it is very special to them. They say that bathing in it brings them good luck.

Stamps: Ordinary stamps in India have a picture of Mahatma Gandhi on them. Some stamps celebrate different parts of Indian life. These stamps show some of its wildlife.

Glossary

curried Flavoured with many spices.

chapatti Circular flat bread, a bit like a thick pancake.

coir Coconut fibres, used to make ropes and sacks.

dosa A thin pancake made from rice or lentils.

harmonium A musical instrument with a keyboard, which the player pumps with air.

Hindi The most important language in India.

idli A sticky ball of food made from ground-up rice.

monsoon The name of the wind that blows over India from the Arabian Sea. It brings a lot of rain.

Onam The most important festival in Kerala. It celebrates the end of the harvest.

private school A school where parents have to pay for their children to study.

sambar A clear soup made from vegetables and lentils.

shrine A sacred place. It can be a building or a special area inside a home.

spice Something that is used to give food a flavour.

state An area within a country which is like a 'mini-country'.

tamarind A fruit with a sour taste.

temple A building in which people pray.

urad dhal A type of lentil, found in most good supermarkets. To make dosas, you could use any type of lentil.

Further Information

Information books:

A Flavour of India by Mike Hirst (Hodder Wayland, 1998)

Geeta's Day by Prodeepta Das (Frances Lincoln, 2000)

I is for India by Prodeepta Das (Frances Lincoln, 1997)

We Come From India by David Cumming (Hodder Wayland, 1999)

Fiction:

Rama and the Demon King by Jessica Southam (Frances Lincoln, 1997)

The Tiger Child by Joanna Troughton (Puffin, 1996)

CD-ROM:

Wake up World! by Beatrice Hollyer (Frances Lincoln/Oxfam, 1999)

Resource packs:

The Clothes Line Activities booklet and photo pack (Oxfam, 1998) Looks at cotton production and the clothing industry in India.

The India File Video and activity booklets, and accompanying book *Celebrating India* (Channel 4 Learning, 1998)

Shompa Lives in India Big book and teacher's booklet (Christian Aid, 1999)

Talking Drum Booklet, photopack and music cassette (Christian Aid/SCIAF, 1996) Includes a traditional story from India.

Thengapalli and *Thengapalli: Forest and Futures* (Hampshire County Council Education, 1997 and 2000) Life in the Indian village of Keshapur.

Websites:

Christian Aid: www.christian-aid.org.uk

Oxfam: www.oxfam.org.uk/coolplanet

Save the Children: www.scfuk.org.uk

Unicef: www.unicef.org.uk

Index